FINAL EXIT FO

MW01709214

MICHAEL VINER

SUSIE DOTAN AND WILL SUCKOW CO-CONSPIRATORS

DOVE
BOOKS

ISBN 0-7871-0564-3

Printed in the United States of America

Dove Books
8955 Beverly Boulevard
West Hollywood, CA 90048

Distributed by Penguin USA

Cover and interior illustrations by Will Suckow

First Printing: September 1996

10 9 8 7 6 5 4 3 2 1

OTHER BOOKS BY THE AUTHOR:

FINAL EXIT FOR LAWYERS

FINAL EXIT FOR BARNEY

FINAL EXIT FOR CATS

FINAL EXIT FOR WATER POLO

FINAL EXIT FOR MARLON BRANDO (AUTOBIOGRAPHY)

FINAL EXIT FOR ROMEO, JULIET, AND MADONNA (A PICTORIAL)

BRIDGES AT MADISON COUNTY - MEMOIRS OF A DENTIST

LINCOLN AT GETTYSBURG - HENRY FORD REMEMBERS

CONGRATULATIONS! YOU'VE JUST ASKED YOURSELF THE MOST INTELLIGENT QUESTION YOU ARE CAPABLE OF. "WHY WOULD WE WANT TO KILL HOCKEY PLAYERS WHEN THEY DO SUCH A GOOD JOB OF IT THEMSELVES?" THE ANSWER IS EASY. AS USUAL, THEIR STRATEGIES ARE USUALLY JUST SLIGHTLY OFF, THEY SLIP UP, THEIR AIM IS BAD, AND THEY TEND TO LEAVE A MESSY TRAIL OF BLOOD IN THEIR WAKE. SO, WE DECIDED TO DO THE JOB FOR THEM. IN THE FOLLOWING PAGES YOU WILL SEE SEVERAL WAYS TO ACHIEVE THEIR ULTIMATE DEMISE, THEIR DECIMATION, THEIR FINAL HUMILIATION, AND, OF COURSE, THEIR FINAL EXIT.

DECLARE BEER ILLEGAL AT ALL GAMES.

REWARD THE STANLEY CUP WINNERS WITH A WEEK IN WINNIPEG. LOSERS GET TWO WEEKS.

SHARPEN THE BUTT END OF THE STICK.

HAVE THE MIGHTY DUCKS FACE-OFF AGAINST THE DONALD DUCKS.

HAVE ROD SERLING SUDDENLY APPEAR IN A ZONE.

PAINT A TARGET ON THE GOALIE'S ATHLETIC CUP.

CANCEL "HOCKEY NIGHT" IN CANADA.

FEED ALL THE PLAYERS POWERBARS BEFORE A GAME.

APPOINT A GOVERNMENT COMMISSION TO OVERSEE HOCKEY.

FORBID GOLF IN THE OFF-SEASON.

IMPOSE A TV BLACKOUT OF ALL HOCKEY GAMES FOR AN ENTIRE SEASON, INCLUDING THE STANLEY CUP PLAYOFFS.

FORCE EACH PLAYER TO UNDERGO PSYCHOTHERAPY FOR THEIR VIOLENT TENDENCIES.

MAKE HANNIBAL LECTER GOALIE.

ALLOW RUSSIAN SPORTS AGENTS TO TAKE OVER THE COLLECTIVE BARGAINING PROCESS.

HAVE THE PLAYERS ARRESTED BY VICE FOR HOOKING.

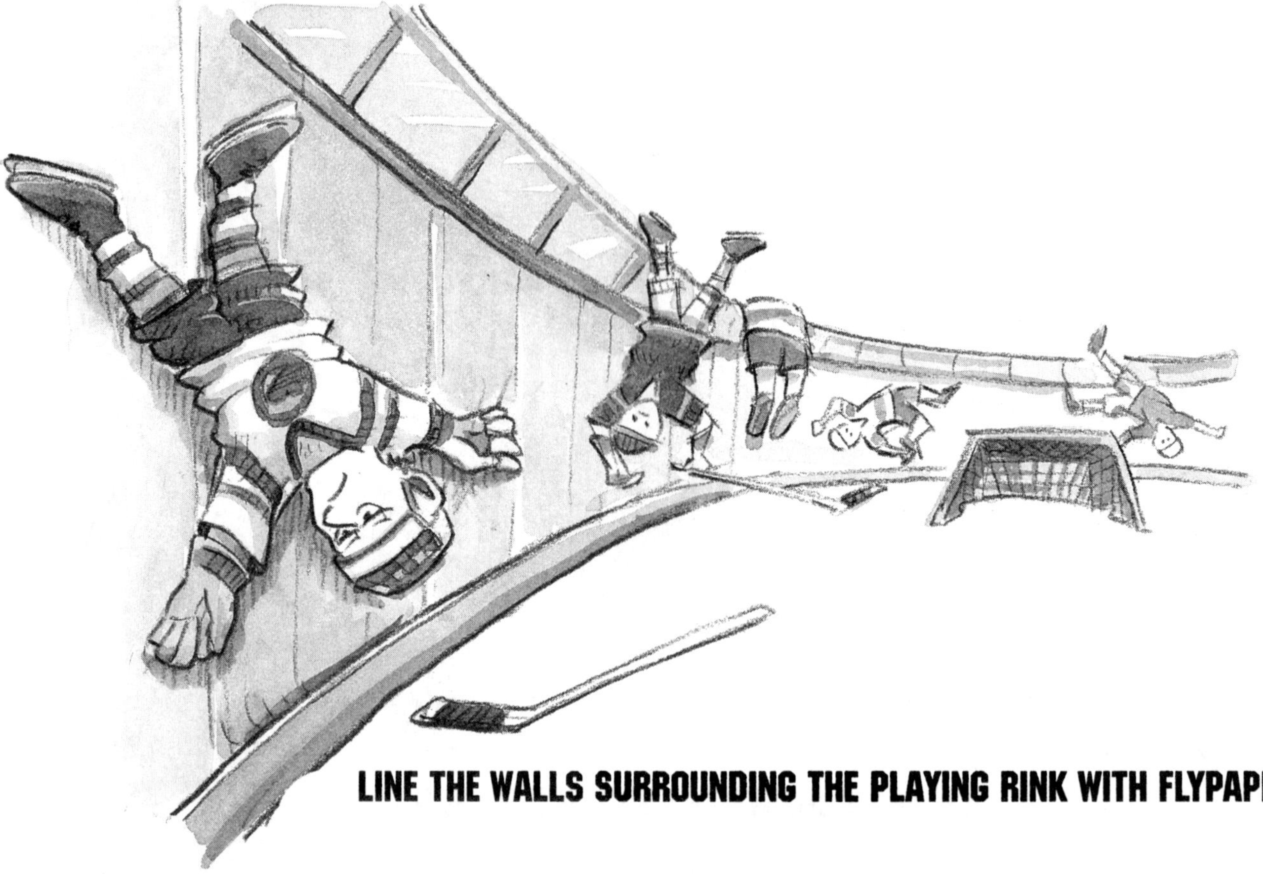

LINE THE WALLS SURROUNDING THE PLAYING RINK WITH FLYPAPER.

OR COAT THE BOARDS THAT LINE THE RINK WITH SANDPAPER.

FORCE ALL THE TEAMS TO UNDERGO A COURSE IN "SOCIAL ETIQUETTE" TAUGHT BY MISS MANNERS.

GIVE MONICA SELES'S CRAZED FAN A PRIME SEAT, AFTER ALLOWING HIM TO EMIGRATE FROM GERMANY.

SEND A DESCENDANT OF THE HUNCHBACK OF NOTRE DAME INTO THE UPPER SCAFFOLDING OF THE MONTREAL FORUM.

FORCE THEM TO WEAR ROLLERBLADES ON THE ICE.

ALLOW LIABILITY LAWYERS TO WORK THE CROWD.

ALLOW SPONSORS TO PRINT THEIR LOGOS IN THE ICE.

AWARD THE REVEREND JIM JONES THE KOOL- AID CONCESSION.

BAN ANYONE WHO'S NAME ENDS IN "ZKY" FROM PLAYING HOCKEY.

PUT TONYA HARDING AND JEFF GILOOLY IN CHARGE OF OFFENSIVE STRATEGIES.

SEND THEM IN TO PLAY A TEAM OF VAMPIRES.

FORCE THE PLAYERS TO CLEAN UP THEIR LANGUAGE AND PENALIZE ANYONE WHO SWEARS. . .

OR ISSUE A PROCLAMATION THAT HOCKEY PLAYERS MUST SWEAR BILINGUALLY.

CITING THE SUCCESS OF FOOTBALL, MAKE BLOCKING AND TACKLING LEGAL IN HOCKEY.

MAKE A RULE THAT DOES NOT ALLOW ANY NAMES, NICKNAMES, OR LOGOS ON TEAM JERSEYS.

STAR MARIO LEMIEUX AND CLAUDE LEMIEUX IN A KITTY LITTER COMMERCIAL.

THEN STICK MARIO IN A SUPER MARIO BROTHERS VIDEO GAME.

INTRODUCE A NEW TRAINING PROGRAM WHICH INCLUDES VEGETARIAN TEAM MEALS AND PREGAME YOGA.

MAKE ALL PLAYERS PAY FOR THEIR OWN DENTAL AND PLASTIC SURGERY BILLS.

DISCOVER AN OLD GEEZER SITTING THERE QUIETLY ICE FISHING IN THE MIDDLE OF A GAME. . .

AND HAVE HIM ACTUALLY CATCH A BIG FISH!

MAKE IT ILLEGAL TO SELL HOCKEY SPORTS MEMORABILIA, ESPECIALLY IN CANADA.

HAVE HUGH GRANT AND DIVINE BROWN GIVE A LECTURE TO THE PLAYERS ON THE BENEFITS OF SAFE SEX.

FORCE THE NETWORKS TO SCHEDULE "HOCKEY NIGHT IN CANADA" ON A WEEKDAY AFTERNOON SO IT COMPETES WITH TALK SHOWS AND SOAPS.

HAVE THE FINNISH FLASH ARRESTED FOR "FLASHING."

MAKE HOCKEY ILLEGAL IN CANADA, AND BAN ALL GAMES.

HAVE ALL THE PLAYERS PENALIZED FOR CROSS-DRESSING WHILE CROSS-CHECKING.

CHOOSE VALUJET AS THE OFFICIAL AIRLINE OF THE NHL.

SUBSTITUTE A GRENADE FOR THE HOCKEY PUCK.

IMPOSE BASIC ACADEMIC REQUIREMENTS ON ALL NHL DRAFTEES.

HIRE SUMO WRESTLERS AS GOALIES.

MAKE JACK THE RIPPER THE OFFICIAL TEAM MASCOT.

SEND THE MOUNTIES IN TO PERFORM A "MUSICAL RIDE ON ICE" BETWEEN PERIODS.

MAKE IT A REQUIREMENT FOR ADMISSION THAT ALL FANS READ "THE GAME" BY KEN DRYDEN.

HIRE DR. FRANKENSTEIN TO BE THE OFFICIAL TEAM PHYSICIAN.

MAKE CANADIAN DOLLARS THE OFFICIAL CURRENCY OF THE NHL.

SCHEDULE THE STANLEY CUP PLAYOFFS TO BE PLAYED IN STANLEY PARK IN THE MIDDLE OF TOURIST SEASON.

SEND AN INSULTING LETTER TO THE HEAD OF THE FORMER SOVIET RED ARMY THANKING HIM FOR ALL THEIR GREAT PLAYERS.

INSTEAD OF MAKING THE HOCKEY STICKS OUT OF EASTON ALUMINUM, MAKE THEM OUT OF CAST IRON.

SEND ALL ENFORCERS TO BRUCE LEE'S MARTIAL ARTS TRAINING SCHOOL.

NAME PETER POCKLINGTON AS DIRECTOR OF LEAGUE STABILITY.

HYPNOTIZE THE PLAYERS ON THE OPPOSING TEAM INTO PERFORMING "SWAN LAKE" DURING A GAME.

MAKE EACH PLAYER SLEEP IN THE SAME ROOM AS HIS SHIN GUARDS. . .

AND INSTRUCT EACH PLAYER TO APPLY HIS SHIN GUARDS USING KRAZY GLUE.

FORCE THE PLAYERS ON THE TORONTO MAPLE LEAFS TO PUT UP A STAND IN THE PARKING LOT AND SELL MAPLE SYRUP EACH TIME THEY LOSE A GAME.

CHANGE THE NAME OF THE TORONTO MAPLE LEAFS TO THE TORONTO FIG LEAFS.

REDESIGN THE UNIFORMS IN APPEALING PASTEL COLORS AND DECORATIVE MOTIFS IN A GESTURE TO ATTRACT MORE FEMALE FANS TO THE SPORT.

SCHEDULE A REMATCH BETWEEN TEAM CANADA AND TEAM RUSSIA—WITHOUT PAUL HENDERSON.

SPREAD THE RUMOR THAT HOCKEY PLAYERS MAKE LOUSY LOVERS.

CHANGE THE RULES TO ALLOW YOUNGER PLAYERS.

REPORT SIGHTINGS OF "THE STRATFORD STREAKER," HOWIE MORENZ, IN DIFFERENT PARTS OF CANADA. START RUMORS THAT HE IS STILL ALIVE AND ON YOUR TEAM.

MAKE THE TEAMS COED.

OPEN THE KENDO SCHOOL OF STICK-HANDLING.

FORCE THE TEAM TO PLAY AGAINST A GROUP OF DISGRUNTLED POSTAL WORKERS.

MAKE A RULE OUTLAWING THE WASHING OF UNIFORMS BETWEEN GAMES.

TELL THE PLAYERS THAT ALL JOKES ABOUT PUCKING ARE OFF LIMITS.

PIT OLD FANS AGAINST NEW FANS IN A FIGHT TO DECIDE THE "ALL-TIME GREAT" PLAYERS.

MAKE WAYNE NETWON THE OFFICIAL ANTHEM SINGER FOR ALL GAMES.

ABOUT THE AUTHOR:

MICHAEL VINER WAS FIRST DISCOVERED IN YELLOWSTONE NATIONAL PARK WHERE HE HAD EVIDENTLY BEEN LEFT BEHIND. HE WAS RAISED BY WOLVES, BUT QUICKLY ADAPTED TO CIVILIZATION AND IN FACT ATTENDED HARVARD UNIVERSITY WHERE HE ACHIEVED A STRAIGHT "A" AVERAGE UNTIL TRAGEDY STRUCK. ON HIS WAY TO HIS GRADUATION CEREMONY, HE WAS RUN OVER WHILE CHASING A CAR. . . BUT HE'S DOING BETTER NOW. . . THANK YOU.

ABOUT THE CO-AUTHORS:

SUSIE DOTAN IS BEST KNOWN BY THOSE WHO CRUISE THE SUNSET STRIP, FOR HER TIGHT CYCLING OUTFIT AND HER ABILITY TO MAKE FRIENDS QUICKLY (NOT TO MENTION HER TALENT FOR MAKING A QUICK BUCK).

WILL SUCKOW IS A TALENTED CARTOONIST AND PORTRAIT ARTIST WHOSE BEST-KNOWN WORK IS OFTEN FEATURED ON "AMERICA'S MOST WANTED", THOUGH NOT IN CONNECTION WITH HIS DRAWINGS.